TAKE CHARGE

GET RESULTS

A simple approach to the Principles of Success.

GEORGE J. MORSE
Personal & Professional Leadership Coach

Published by Morse & Associates, Inc.
Oscoda, Michigan

Published by:
Morse & Associates, Inc.
101-3 River Rd., P.O. Box 695
Oscoda, MI 48750
(989) 739-3847
www.coachmorse.com

Cover design, and interior layout, done in coordination with
    All-in-one Design: www.allinonedesign.com
Interior graphics by Deborah Reynolds
Cover photo by James O'Briant

Library of Congress Control Number: 2005910140

ISBN 0-9774877-0-9

Printed in the United States by Morris Publishing
3212 East Highway 30
Kearney, NE 68847
1-800-650-7888

DEDICATION

To my children,

Michelle
A.J.
&
Taylor Marie

My love for you has no boundaries. You are my hope,
my joy, and my inspiration. I could not ask for, nor
receive a greater gift than you.

This book is for you. I hope it helps you find the kind of
success you're looking for, as you sail toward the
realization of your dreams.

To my wife,

Andrea

My "hard-headed woman",
Thank you for loving me, for being my partner, and
sharing yourself with me in all things.
I love you.

CONTENTS

ACKNOWLEDGMENTS

I would like to thank my parents, George H. Morse and Lorna Morse, for giving me a true sense of what it means to be successful by demonstrating a way of life focused on responsibility, thoughtfulness, kindness, and generosity. Though I know what they gave me was intended as a gift, I cannot help but feel indebted to them. For their undying love and encouragement, I remain forever grateful.

I want to give special thanks to my Regional Manager, Stephanie Zeilinger, for acting as a sounding board for my ideas, and providing honest feedback at every stage of the book's development. She helped me follow through on my commitment to write a book that was easy to read, and easy to understand. I can't thank her enough.

I would also like to thank those, who took the time to read my manuscript at various stages in the editing process, and who shared their reactions and opinions with regard to both content and grammar. Their encouragement and constructive criticism not only helped me maintain the confidence I needed to see the project through, but greatly enhanced the quality of the book as well. Thanks (listed in alphabetical order) to: Gary Conklin, Jennifer Huebel, Jim Kitch, Paul Knapp, James Magadini, Paul Mayville and the management team at Northland Credit Union, George & Lorna Morse, Michelle Morse, Mary Reitler, Bob Stalker, George Thompson, Jim Winner, and Stephanie Zeilinger.

Finally, I want to thank my managers and their respective teams for their outstanding performance. Without their loyalty, dedication, and contribution to the company, this book would not have been written. I thank them all: Denise Zeilinger and the Auburn team, Misty Pelo and the Essexville team, Jessica Zeilinger and the Lafayette team, Mary Palmer and the Oscoda team, and Stephanie Zeilinger and the Wilder team. Here's to their continued success!

In Times Like These

In times like these
We are tested. Pushed to the limits of what is possible,
And beyond;
Desperate to see the future, as the present
Blocks our view.

In times like these
We are tested. Pressed to find the answers in a never-
ending
Sea of questions;
Fighting to keep our backs off the wall, just as life would
Have us against it.

In times like these
We are arrested. Failing to elude the freezing
Winds of fear;
Bound in chains, as prisoners of our own
Self-doubt.

In times like these
We are bested. More inclined to blame than
Find solutions;
More inclined to give up, and
Make excuses.

In times like these
We are tested.
Make or break,
Win or Lose,
Pass or Fail.

INTRODUCTION

Many people in our world today are struggling. Young people, old people, and the middle-aged alike, are struggling to find purpose and meaning in their lives. Many are just struggling to get by. Families, Communities, Schools, Governments, and Companies are struggling to find leadership, and to achieve great results. Many are just struggling to get by.

Finding success in life or business doesn't have to be such a struggle. Success can be achieved by anyone who seeks it. Where to look for and how to find success, are outlined within these pages. *Take Charge – Get Results* describes a process that when followed, will help you, the reader, find the kind of success you're looking for.

The Success Principles discussed in this book are not new, however the way in which they are presented *is* new. You'll find the information relevant, easy to read, and easy to understand. From the first chapter to the last you will see a natural progression, and gain a deeper appreciation for how the successful application, of one principle, positively impacts your readiness to apply the next.

Whatever you hope to achieve for your life, business or organization, follow this process from beginning to end. Define success on your own terms. Make a decision to lead. Unleash your desire by creating a vision (what you want and why). Tap into your source of inspiration. Establish your goals. Sustain your motivation. Make a lasting commitment. Plan your work. Implement your plan. Solve problems along the way. Keep your balance. And finally, take ownership of your results. Anyone can achieve success once they know how. So can you.

I hope you enjoy reading this book, and will use it as a resource to help you find the kind of success you're looking for. I wish you all the best on your journey, as you discover how to *Take Charge*, and *Get Results*.

TAKE CHARGE
GET RESULTS

Chapter One

SUCCESS REDEFINED

"You won't get far up the mountain wearing size nine boots if your feet are size ten."

What does it mean to be successful? - To have a high paying job, to live in a great big fancy house, to drive an expensive car, to go on vacation every year, to own a yacht, to have a summer house? Is that what it means? - To have a family, to have a good paying job, to drive an SUV, to live in a nice house, to volunteer in your community, to vacation sometimes, to own a boat and snowmobiles? Is that what it means? - To be a Doctor, Lawyer, CEO, Senator or President? Is that what it means? - To be a Movie-Star, Professional Athlete, Recording Artist or an Author perhaps? Is that what it means to be successful?

Look Below the Surface

Sometimes I hear people say, "Look at him, he's so successful!" or "Look at her, she's so successful!" to which I usually respond something like, "Really? What makes you think that?" They usually give an answer like, "Well, he has a beautiful wife, beautiful children, a beautiful dog, he lives in a nice house, he has a great job, and he takes his family on vacation... Oh, just look at him. He has success written all over him!"

But can success really be measured by what we see? If so, what about the man who has a beautiful wife, but is on his third marriage, the one whose beautiful child is in rehab, whose beautiful dog isn't house broken, who lives in a nice house that has been refinanced for 125% of its appraised value, who puts in 60 hours a week at the office, and who needs a week to recover from every vacation? Is he really successful? If you're thinking, "Well of course he's not successful," good for you.

It's important for us to understand on the surface, a person can appear to be successful, but the true story of success is told far below the surface, where no one else can see. Many people appear to be successful, but are they really?

If we can't see success, how can it be measured? Very simply put, if you are going to measure success in your own life, you have to define what success means for you. Base your definition on what you think, not what society thinks or what you see on television; not what your mother, brother, sister, father, aunt, uncle, cousin or spouse thinks – not what your boss, teacher, pastor, counselor, neighbor or friend thinks, but what you think.

Think back to the last time you accomplished something you felt good about. Who was the first one to know you succeeded? You were. Now think back to the last time you felt disappointed when your attempts, to accomplish something, were unsuccessful. Who was the first one to know you failed? That's right, you were. You are the only one who knows what's going on beneath the surface of your life, so your definition of success must be specific to your own situation.

Get Your Priorities Straight

As you move forward, contemplating your success, and as you begin to make decisions that will start you on your way, take care to make decisions that are consistent with your definition of success. Set your priorities, and avoid decisions that create problems.

The following story illustrates my point.

Mike had always wanted to own a Corvette. It was on his "Things I Want" list, but something he couldn't afford. Every time Mike saw a Corvette he would say, "One of these days, I'm going to have one of those." For Mike, owning a Corvette symbolized success. Oh sure, Mike had a wife, children, a house and a pretty good job. He had other dreams and goals associated with those areas of his life too, but that car... that car would be awesome!

Mike used to spend time every day, dreaming of that car. He could see himself racing down the highway, wind in his hair; king of the open road. He could see himself cruising through town, turning heads left and right. He could even hear the people say, "Wow, look at that car! Who's that driving? Is that Mike? It is! It's Mike! He is so successful!" After he finished daydreaming, Mike would crunch the numbers again, figuring out how much money he needed to afford his dream car.

Then, one day Mike got a promotion at work, and a big enough pay increase (if he juggled a few other personal finances) to afford the payments on a new Corvette. Like many people, Mike had no shortage of things to spend the extra money on; important things, like increasing IRA contributions, saving for college tuition, new shingles for the roof and paying off a high interest credit card. However, like so many people before him have done, Mike chose to spend his extra income on the car he had always wanted.

The day Mike drove it off the lot, he felt like a million bucks. "Look at me!" he thought, "I've made it!" And so he had. Hadn't he? Well, no. Not really.

What happened as a result of Mike's decision to buy that car was nothing short of disaster. First of all, Mike's celebration of success quickly came to an end the moment he pulled into the driveway and his wife saw the car. He spent the next three hours vehemently defending his decision, and the next three days sleeping on the couch.

To add to his problems, Mike had miscalculated the costs of insurance and extra gas needed to get back and forth from work. His miscalculation meant that all of Mike's monthly income was now being used to pay bills, and for the first time since he was a college student, Mike found himself living paycheck to paycheck. As the roof began to leak, and the credit cards reached their limit, and his marriage began to suffer, Mike began to realize that his decision to buy the car had been a mistake (although technically it was a goal of his, and people did say, "Wow look at Mike!").

Even though he appeared to be successful, Mike didn't feel successful. In fact, his decision to buy something he thought would make him look successful to others, had brought about multiple failures in other areas of his life. When Mike really thought about it, he knew those other areas meant more to him than any car ever could.

When you make decisions, remember our friend Mike, and carefully consider how those decisions affect the other areas of your life. If the achievement of one goal causes problems and set-backs in your life, you need to re-examine your priorities and redefine what success means to you. Success begets success; if you successfully achieve a goal in one area of your life, it will compliment and support your continued success in other areas.

Define Success on Your Own Terms

In today's World, many people chase after success, trying to have, do, or be what someone else has, does, or is; only to discover, once they've arrived, they don't feel successful at all. They will readily admit on the outside, they have success "written all over them", but on the inside they, often times, feel empty and unfulfilled. Why? It's because they used someone else's definition of success, instead of their own. You won't get far up the mountain wearing size nine boots if your feet are size ten.

Regardless of the success you are looking for, whether in your career, business, group, organization, or personal life, it is vital that you define your own terms for that success. What is important to you is unique to your own set of circumstances. Your career goals, the mission of your business, group or organization, your relationships, family, friends, hobbies all are reliant on your understanding of what you hope to achieve. Success in these areas is impossible to gauge by any other view but your own.

Before you set out on your journey to succeed, make sure you're wearing the right sized boots. Redefine the meaning of success for you, in your own life. Shut out everything you've heard and everything you've seen, and listen to what your insides tell you.

What size boots do *you* wear? What does success mean to you? What are you looking for in life? What do you want, and what's important to you? What is *your* definition of success?

Chapter Two

UNDERSTANDING LEADERSHIP

"It is Leadership that sets the course, and provides direction for all achievement, great or small."

Over the years, leadership has been defined, re-defined, debated, discussed, and analyzed. It has been dissected into styles, forms, varying degrees, principles, character traits, and responsibilities. Despite all of the expert analysis, the question, "What is Leadership?" remains, in large part, unanswered. If you ask a thousand people what leadership is, you will get a thousand different answers. The answer is lost, somewhere deep within a thick cloud of confused opinion, theory and conjecture. The existence of real leadership in our society, our organizations, our families and our lives has been lost, somewhere in the attempted application of ingenious new techniques and half-baked notions.

What Leadership Is

Leadership belongs to the family of universal truth, and its meaning cannot be changed every time an authority figure feels the need to abdicate his or her responsibility. Leadership has only one meaning: to be responsible for all outcomes, whether successful or failed, anytime, all of the time. Leadership is what it is, and a person either understands it or does not; either employs its principles or does not. There is no such thing as "good leadership" or "bad leadership", only 'leadership" or "no leadership". The existence of leadership is evidenced by the existence of followers. No followers – no leadership. It's that simple.

What Leadership Is Not

Just because you pay somebody to work for you, and they do what you tell them to does not make them your follower, just as your working for someone and following their orders, does not make them your leader. In our society today, many businesses, governmental agencies and organizations are confusing the issuance and following of orders with the existence of leadership. You can pay someone to follow your orders, but you cannot pay someone to follow *you*. It is the misconception, or poor understanding of what leadership really is, that causes most of the problems for these groups, such as discontented workers, low morale, inefficiency and high turnover, to name a few.

More often than not, the authority figures of these groups attempt to improve morale and increase productivity by increasing pay and benefits. However, when the desired result is not achieved, and the price of obedience becomes too costly, they resort to threats of demotion, reduction in benefits or termination of employment. With the adoption of this "Get results or else" policy, they actually create a toxic, fear based environment. The responsibility for poor performance is shifted completely off of the authority figures' shoulders onto the shoulders of their employees. While this approach may bring about short-term improvements in performance, it ignores the serious lack of leadership, and has long-term consequences. It's the absence of leadership which ultimately results in decreased performance as employees spend more and more time preparing their resumes.

[I'm not suggesting that authority figures can't hold a subordinate accountable for performance. On the contrary, they can and they should, however responsibility for overall results rests squarely in the lap of those in authority, a fact that any real leader understands; a responsibility that any real leader accepts.]

Accept Responsibility

For success in any endeavor, leadership must be present, because it is leadership that sets the course, and provides direction for all achievement, great or small. In order to establish the existence of leadership (that is, the existence of followers) one must have a proper understanding of its most basic purpose.

The primary responsibility of leadership is to take charge, or more accurately to take charge of; to care for, to be responsible for, to take into one's care (or charge). A leader has a responsibility to care for those in his or her charge. The common expectations and principles of Leadership – to lead, to guide, to enlighten, to direct, and to inspire action, – all stem from a leader's acceptance of this primary responsibility to take charge.

[It is important to note that "taking charge" is different from "being in charge."]

Being in charge, by virtue of position, has no bearing on leadership, in and of itself. Anyone can be placed in charge of something or someone, but that doesn't make them a leader. Instead, leadership begins with a decision to accept the primary responsibility of a leader: to take charge, to care for – to be responsible for the success and well being of something or someone, for example, a situation, personal goal, project, marriage, family, group, or business.

Take Charge

You may be wondering, "What does leadership have to do with me? I'm not in charge of anything or anyone." Well, yes you are. In the most basic sense, we are all in charge of something or someone – ourselves. That's right. You are in charge, of you. You are responsible for you. The real question is: Are you merely "in charge" or have you "taken charge?"

Leadership plays just as important a role in our personal lives as it does in our professional lives, and is a necessary element to achieving our goals. If you are struggling with performance, getting poor results, or experiencing failure in some area of your life or business, do not ignore the true cause of the problem (lack of leadership).   Do not shift responsibility onto someone else's shoulders.

If you are going to get results, you must take responsibility, by *taking charge* of yourself and your situation.   Make a decision to accept this primary responsibility of Leadership.   Invoke its power in your own life. Set a course for success. Take charge, and lead yourself and your followers – your organization, business, community, family – to greatness.

Chapter Three

UNLEASH YOUR DESIRE

"It is the understanding of who you are that helps kindle the fire of desire deep within you."

Everyone has desire and uses it to get what they want to some extent or another. Desire is the wanting of something. To want, wish for, long for or yearn for something; that is what desire means. Desire is a powerful emotion, that when properly focused, can drive one to excel and achieve uncommon results.

Desire and Winning

We have all witnessed the power of desire at one time or another. Have you ever watched a sporting event – football, basketball, soccer or a boxing match perhaps? Have you ever heard the trainer telling his boxer, "You have to want it more than he does!" or the coach yelling to his players, "Who wants it more?" Have you ever seen an underdog win a competition, astounding and inspiring you and the crowd? Sure you have. You may have even thought, or heard someone say, "He wanted it more than the other guy," or "They lost, because they just didn't want it bad enough." When the subject of desire is approached in this context, it is quite easy for all of us to understand. When it comes to sports, desire has a clear impact on winning.

The same understanding, of how desire affects winning in sports, can be applied when considering our own possibility for success. Desire affects winning in all areas of life. The challenge for you is to recognize the desire within you. Focus on what you want and unleash your desire, allowing the power it creates to assist you as you work toward the realization of your dreams.

Raise Your Self-Awareness

All great achievement is fueled by desire – a deep and powerful, *burning* desire. You can't go outside yourself to find desire, and nobody can give it to you. Desire comes from within; derived from your knowledge and understanding of the "who, what and why" of your being.

Who are you and who do you want to be? What do you want to have and what do you want to create? Why are you the way you are? Why do you want the things you want, and why are they important to you?

By answering these and other questions you will begin to improve your self-awareness and deepen your understanding. It is this understanding of who you are that helps kindle the fire of desire deep within you, and it is *your* desire that will serve as the basis for all your future achievement. To successfully unleash the power of desire you must begin by raising your self-awareness.

To strengthen your self-awareness you must look inward and ask yourself questions; thought provoking questions that force you to look deep inside. Search long and hard. The answers are there within you. Here are some questions to help you get started (write down your answers). Answering these and other self-probing questions honestly, will raise your awareness, deepen your understanding, and assist you in discovering what drives you.

- Who am I?
- Why am I here?
- What is my purpose?
- What do I feel compelled to do?
- Why do I act the way I do?
- What do I want and why? (things)
- What do I want and why? (relationship)
- What do I want and why? (family)
- What do I want and why? (career)
- Why are they important to me?
- Am I happy?
- Am I satisfied?
- Am I fulfilled?
- What would make me happy, satisfied and fulfilled? (Or complete?)
- What do I love to do?
- Is there anything I feel passionate about?
- What is my dream?
- What am I afraid of?
- Why am I afraid of it?
- What do I really want to create in my life?

- What is stopping me from getting what I want and why?

Develop a Clear Vision

Now that you've spent some time looking inward, asking and answering questions, you should be able to see an image taking shape or a picture forming in your mind of how you want your life to be. That is your vision, and in order to fully access the power of desire, it needs to be clearly and vividly developed. Take some time now and describe your vision in writing. Yes, write it down. What do you want to be? What do you want to have? How do you want to feel? What matters most and why? It is vision that ultimately unlocks the door to desire, and the clearer the vision, the more powerful the desire.

Below is my vision for my business. I've included it here, to give you an idea of what your clearly developed vision could look like. It contains what I'm trying to build or create, how I want to go about doing that, and incorporates core values that I feel are important for me to uphold. I keep it posted where I can see it every day, and it helps keep my desire *red-hot*.

Vision: To build a company that provides opportunity, security and stability for employees, by focusing on sound operations, growth, diversification, and creating a corporate culture that values individuals and recognizes the importance of their contribution to the company.

[Now it's your turn. Do yourself a favor and invest some time developing *your* vision. It's important.]

Chapter Four

FINDING INSPIRATION

*"When you focus on the achievement of a goal, move with
a sense of purpose toward its fulfillment, and establish
your intent, then solutions or ideas that at one time didn't
seem to exist will just come to you. That's Inspiration."*

Once you've established and unleashed your
powerful desire to succeed, the plans you make and the
ideas you come up with must be equally as powerful;
ideas that send you and others running around the room,
jumping up and down, or banging your fist on the table
and shouting, "Eureka! .... Brilliant! .... What a great idea!
.... Where did that come from? .... I didn't know you were
so smart!" or, "That idea smacks of Genius!" Inspiration
is the key to developing powerful ideas that "smack of
genius", create excitement, and motivate you and others
to act.

In order for you to access your own source of
inspiration, for the creation of those ideas, you must do
two things; move with a sense of purpose, and develop a
strong intent. Purpose is the focused pursuit of a single
goal, while intent is the decision to act. To unlock the
door to inspired thought, to tap into your genius within,
you must do both.

Move With a Sense of Purpose

Have you ever lost or misplaced your car keys? After you searched in all the normal places, as well as in the freezer and inside the oven (to include the broiler pan), and after your check of the drawers (for the third time) produced no result, did you get really frustrated, raise your voice, stomp your feet or repeatedly throw your hands skyward? You may have even stated, defiantly, "I'm not leaving here until I find those keys!" and then, of course, you realized that you couldn't leave without the keys, because you needed them to start your car.

Did you vow to find the keys even "if it killed you?" Or that you would find those keys "if it's the last thing you do" (which it usually ends up being)? Maybe you vowed to find those keys even if you had to "tear the place apart?"

Would you say you became focused on finding those keys? Or that you had a single-minded, concentrated focus and fixation on finding those keys, no matter what the odds, and no matter what you had to do in order to find them? Would you say you were on a *mission* to find those keys, or that you had a sense of *purpose*?

Once your purpose was clear, would you say that your intent was so strong that you made your decision to find those keys "no matter what?" Was your house or apartment spared total destruction by some inspired thought (divine intervention perhaps)?

[I love to hear "key finding" stories. They usually end up going something like this, "…I was so determined to find those keys that I was about to rip the house apart. Then it came to me (inspired idea); as I was getting a box from the back seat, I might have dropped the keys on the floor. Sure enough, when I looked, that's where they were!"]

In this example the "inspired idea" was only received once the purpose (focused pursuit of a single goal) to find those keys was established, and the intention, or decision to act was made to find those keys "no matter what". This is a simple example, but the lesson applies to any situation; when you focus on the achievement of a goal, move with a sense of purpose toward its fulfillment, and establish your intent, then solutions or ideas that at one time didn't seem to exist will just come to you. That's Inspiration.

Make a Decision to Act

Most people don't have much difficulty establishing their purpose, or focusing on a goal they would like to achieve. However, when it comes to developing a strong intent, most people fall short. Making a decision to act is a process, and most people stop just short of making that crucial decision to take action. Not for lack of willingness – they certainly want to take action – but for lack of knowledge. They don't understand the process.

The process of making a decision to take action has three simple steps:

1. Identify the goal to be achieved.

2. Generate a list of ideas; what you could or should do to achieve your goal.

3. Turn your list of what you "could" do into what you "will" do.

Most people stop after the second step and that's why they can never quite seem to follow through or stick with anything long enough to see it achieved. It seems simple enough, but it's amazing how many people out there are sitting on a stack of unachieved goals, complete with lists of all the things they *could* do to achieve them. The only thing standing in the way of action is the completion of their decision making process, to turn what they could do into what they will do.

Based on your desire, to realize what you've envisioned, and your mission (*purpose*) to achieve the goals that support the fulfillment of your vision, establish your *intent* by asking yourself the following questions:

- What am I willing to do?
- What will I do?
- When will I do it?
- Will I do it for as long as it takes?

Key words: I / WILL / DO

How deeply you desire what you want, how focused you are on achieving your goals, and your determination to act on your intentions (what you will do), all have a profound impact on the quality of your ideas. The more creative and brilliant your ideas become, the more inspiring they will be to you and to others.

Chapter Five

GOAL SETTING

"View your goals simply as a list of tasks you will accomplish to realize your vision."

You didn't honestly think you were going to read a book about success and get away without having to focus on goal setting, did you? If you've heard it once, you've heard it a thousand times, "If you want to be successful, you must have clearly defined goals". In our society today, the word "goal" is loosely thrown about, and is consistently over-used, misused and misunderstood. It has almost as many different meanings as there are people on the planet. Goals are critical to great achievement, should be well defined and written, yet, when asked, most people will tell you they have not established any goals, or they have goals, but not in writing.

The first time someone asked me what my goals were (because I insisted I had some, just not written) my response went something like this, "Well ...umm ...uh ...I ...uh ...well ...I ...umm ...well ...uh ...I know what I want." Afterwards, I felt pretty embarrassed, but I got the message; I really didn't know what I wanted, so I went to work on my goals right away. However, like most people, I didn't have a good concept of what goals were, how to go about setting them, defining them, or how to achieve them. To me, the whole process was grueling, and for a number of years the mere mention of the word "goal" would send me running out of the room.

Keep it Simple

What I've learned is this: goal setting is easy once you understand the difference between a goal and a vision. Most people understand goals to be a list of wants, but as we discussed earlier, "wants" are what we use to create a clear vision. Your vision is what you want. A goal is a task that, when completed, brings you closer to the realization of your vision (simply put – something you will do). Be careful not to confuse what you "can do" with what you "will do". What you "can do" is an idea. What you "will do" is a goal.

A soccer coach who wants his team to become State Champions within three years has a vision for his team (to become State Champs). The coach must then, lay out a plan; a list of things to be done (goals to be achieved) that will support the fulfillment of his vision. For example:

In order to realize my vision I will:

1. Recruit and retain strong athletes
2. Increase player strength, speed and stamina
3. Increase player skill level
4. Strengthen team unity
5. Improve communication on the field
6. Develop effective defensive and offensive team strategies

In this example, the coach has begun a list of goals. Once the list is complete, the coach will need to make another list of tasks that support the achievement of each goal. For example:

1. Recruit and retain strong athletes

    *   Attend other sports events to identify candidates for recruitment
    *   Approach candidates to set meeting time to discuss their participation in soccer
    *   Meet with candidates to share vision and outline benefits of participation
    *   Support players' needs both on and off the field
    *   Introduce players to college coaches
    *   Provide scholarship information
    *   Take the team to see a Pro game

In this example the coach has generated a list of specific tasks to support the accomplishment of his first goal. That's all there is to it. Goal setting is only as complicated as you make it. So remember to keep it simple.

Outline Your Success

Now it's your turn to set some goals. View your goals simply as a list of tasks you will accomplish to realize your vision. Go back over your vision (chapter 3), then start by listing six main goals that will support the fulfillment of your vision. Ask yourself, "What does the realization of my vision depend on?" then list the top 6 answers:

1. _____

_____

2. _____

_____

3. _____

_____

4. _____

_____

5. _____

_____

6. _____

_____

Next, write down three or four tasks you will accomplish to support the achievement of each goal. Ask yourself, "What does the achievement of this goal depend on?" When you finish this exercise, you will have an outline for success that will aid you in the development of your strategic plan (we will cover Strategic Planning a little later in the book). An outlining format I like to use is shown below. Any style will work; just remember to keep it simple.

Vision: (state your vision here)

Goals that will support the realization of my vision are:

1. *Goal (first main goal here)*
   a) *Task (necessary to achieve goal)*
   b) *Task*
   c) *Task*
   d) *Task*
2. *Goal*
   a) *Task*
   b) *Task*
   c) *Task*
3. *Goal*
   a) *Task*
   b) *Task*
   c) *Task*
   d) *Task*

RECAP

Congratulations! You're well on your way. Pat yourself on the back and take a look at what you've done so far. So far, you have:

1. Looked at what's going on below the surface of your life.
2. Set your Priorities.
3. Defined Success on your own terms.
4. Deepened your understanding of Leadership.
5. Accepted the responsibility of Leadership.
6. Decided to Take Charge.
7. Recognized your Desire.
8. Raised your Self-Awareness.
9. Developed a clear Vision.
10. Unleashed your Desire.
11. Established a Sense of Purpose.
12. Developed a strong Intent.
13. Established your own source of Inspiration.
14. Identified the main goals that will support the realization of your vision.
15. Identified tasks that will support the accomplishment of your goals.
16. Created an Outline for your Success.

Good for you!!!

Take a moment and allow yourself to feel good. You have just done what most people never will, and the fact that you are still here reading, is proof that you have what it takes to be successful. It sets you apart from nearly everyone else, and you should feel proud of yourself!

Chapter Six

SUSTAINING MOTIVATION

"The key to sustaining motivation is staying focused on your vision, and remaining firmly entrenched in your belief that all things are possible."

As mentioned in chapter four, the more brilliant your ideas become, the more inspiring they will be to you and others. Inspiration provides the foundation for motivation, because the creation of brilliant and powerful ideas fosters in us the belief in possibilities. As our belief grows, so does our motivation. Simply stated, great ideas have the power to inspire and motivate us. How motivated we become, and how long we stay motivated will determine how much we ultimately achieve.

An example of a powerful idea that motivates people to take action is "The American Dream". The notion that a common man or woman can rise from the dust and disadvantage of their surroundings, and raise their station in life – even to become independently wealthy or socially prominent – is a powerful and inspiring idea; so much so that every day it motivates millions to take action in pursuit of that dream.

Just as the idea of the American Dream serves as motivation for many, so too can your ideas serve as motivation for you. You can develop equally powerful and inspiring ideas that will foster the belief in possibilities for your own life. This belief, combined with your clear vision, well-defined goals and strategic plan, will provide you with motivation. Your motivation will make it possible for you to get up day after day, roll up your sleeves, and go to work building your dream.

Believe In the Possible

Believing in possibilities is the force that sustains motivation. It is often referred to as the "power of possibility thinking", and if you are going to sustain your own personal motivation for any length of time, you must believe in the possibility of your own success. You must believe what one person can do another can do. You must believe what is possible for someone else is possible for you. Without this belief, self-doubt will grow within you and rob you of your motivation. Consider the following:

A young Business Manager was having a problem at work. She related to me that her corporate headquarters had always conducted monthly evaluations of the operation of her store, but for whatever reason, the evaluations had become stringent, and in her view, down right nit-picky. The manager began to fail evaluations, and was cited for critical violations of corporate policy, which she felt were nothing more than technicalities.
At first she accepted the increased scrutiny as something she would have to live with, and developed strategies to correct the deficiencies and prevent future problems. The following month, the manager had a

successful evaluation, however the next month she was cited for violations in yet another area; one that had never been a problem in the past.

During regional management meetings, she discovered that other store managers, while sharing her aggravation, were not failing as many of their evaluations as she was. She began to doubt her own ability. The following month, the manager failed her corporate evaluation again, this time being cited for new, as well as, recurring violations.

In the course of the manager relating her story to me, and my asking various, clarifying questions, it became evident that she was close to giving up. I discovered two problems she was having that had all but destroyed her motivation; she had lost sight of why it was important for her to succeed, and she had lost confidence in her ability to pass another evaluation (she didn't believe she could do what the other managers were doing, so maybe she wasn't good enough). When I asked her why she was cited for a recurring violation in an area she demonstrated success with in the past, she said, "Well they (meaning corporate evaluators) are just going to find something wrong anyway, so why bother?"

[Have you ever felt the way she did?]

Having experienced similar feelings myself, I asked her to answer her own question, "Why bother?" We began to go over all the reasons why she should "bother." Why it was important that she make the extra effort to pass her evaluations, and why it was worth doing. As it turned out, she had a long list of very good reasons.

I then asked the manager about her confidence moving forward, encouraged her to tell me of past successes, and had her compare herself to other managers (how they were succeeding where she was not). It wasn't long before she was able to re-establish her belief that she was capable (if they could do it, so could she), and that the possibility of success did, in fact, exist for her.

Once this business manager refocused on what she wanted and why it was important (her vision), what she needed to do (her goals), made a decision to act (her intent), and reaffirmed her belief that she could do it (possibility thinking), she was able to re-fill her motivation tanks, roll up her sleeves and go back to work building her dream. Today, this manager boasts double-digit sales increases, and can't remember the last time she failed an evaluation.

Stay focused

The achievement of your goals is dependent on the action you take. Whether or not you take action, how much you get done, and how long you continue to work are all dependent on your level of motivation and your ability to sustain that motivation. In the previous example, the manager suffered repeated failures, lost sight of why her success was important, and began to doubt herself and her ability. The result was less effort, less attention to detail, less concern for results, and increased failure; all caused by the loss of motivation.

Fortunately, she was able to regain her motivation after having lost it, but it would have been better if she hadn't lost her motivation in the first place. Losing, then finding motivation, then losing and finding it again, is very common and something that most people struggle with. There is a way, however, to break the cycle, and through practice develop the ability to sustain motivation. Staying focused on your vision is crucial to that development. Your vision is the answer to the question, "Why bother?"

If the young manager had stayed focused (rather than having to refocus) on her vision, and had reaffirmed her belief in the possibilities by reminding herself of past success, she could have sustained her motivation (instead of losing it). Instead of almost giving up, she could have overcome the obstacles much easier, and with a higher degree of success.

The next time you feel unmotivated, and wonder why you should bother, think about this manager's story and apply the lesson her experience teaches. The key to sustaining motivation is staying focused on your vision, and remaining firmly entrenched in your belief that all things are possible.

Chapter Seven

MAKING A COMMITMENT

"The key to making a strong and lasting commitment is to take the option of quitting off the table."

Unlike intent, which is the decision to take action, commitment is the decision to continue taking action until your vision is realized – until what you intend to create is completed. Your commitment is what keeps you from giving up. If you have a vision for your life, business or organization, and have established a deep desire, created inspiring ideas, have a sense of purpose, a strong intention, set goals, believe in the possibility of your success and are motivated, the only thing left to do is make a commitment to see it through. You might be thinking, "Oh yes, I'm committed", but if your strategic plan ends with the words, "…and if this doesn't work I can do something else", then you are not truly committed.

There will be a Test

At some point in everyone's life they will encounter a problem that appears to be unsolvable, or one of such gravity that it would seem all is lost; one that will leave them with an overwhelming sense of hopelessness and despair. In times like these a person's commitment is tested, and whether they pass or fail, when the test is over, they will know the true meaning of commitment. They will understand how their commitment or lack thereof contributed to their success or failure.

This may have already happened in your life. You may have been on the passing side or the failing side of the test, or maybe you have yet to be tested. In any case, when you work toward the realization of your dreams, the bigger the vision, the harder your test is bound to be; and believe me, you will be tested.

The good news is that by deepening your understanding of commitment today, you can pass the tests you will face tomorrow; thus allowing you to find solutions and overcome obstacles, so you can effectively stay your course.

Take quitting, off the Table

The key to making a strong and lasting commitment is to take the option of quitting off the table. When you are faced with obstacles and looking for solutions to overcome them, you will end up with several options to choose from. For most people, giving up is always an option (they won't admit that, but it's true. The bottom line: people frequently exercise the option to quit). It's better to just take the option of quitting off the table.

About ten years into my marriage, my wife and I were having real trouble. Actually, trouble is an understatement! Even the marriage counselor told me our situation was hopeless, and she recommended we get divorced. Feeling there was no other choice, I filed for divorce. It was the worst time of my life. My failing business didn't seem very important compared to the prospect of losing my family, and there didn't seem to be anything I could do to save either one. I had almost completely given up (about ready to fail my commitment test) when my mother gave me a little advice; a few simple, but powerful words that not only saved my marriage, but had a major impact on all areas of my life.

My mother told me how at one point, in her marriage of forty years, my father and she were arguing frequently. The subject of divorce came up often, until it seemed they couldn't have a disagreement without mentioning divorce. I asked her how they overcame the problem, and her answer was simple. She told me that both of them knew they did not want a divorce. They loved each other and desired to stay together, so they decided to stop throwing divorce on the table as an option. Once they stopped considering divorce as an option they had no other choice but to find ways to get along and find solutions to their problems.

My wife and I followed my mother's advice to take divorce off the table as an option, and it has made all the difference in our marriage. It has been more than ten years since we reconciled our differences, and as I write this, our 20th Wedding Anniversary is only one month away. Sure, we've had our share of arguments along the way, but we've worked through them together and found solutions that worked. Quitting was no longer an option.

In my business I have applied this same understanding of commitment, and the results have been amazing. The turning point in the success of my business was made the day I took quitting off my table as an option. I scribbled out the last line of my plan that said, "…and if this doesn't work I can do something else." I no longer considered finding a different job, selling the business, or filing for bankruptcy as possible solutions to my business woes. Instead of spending valuable time and energy on new exit strategies, I began to focus that energy on the development of new and innovative ways to succeed. As a result, I began to find solutions and grow the business.

Today when I encounter problems, quitting is no longer an option. I only consider options that bring me closer to the realization of my vision. When working with clients, I encourage them to do the same. For those of them who have embraced the concept, the results have been life changing.

MOVING FORWARD

If you haven't done so yet, get a clear picture of your vision and write it down. Write down the goals that support the fulfillment of your vision and the tasks that support the achievement of your goals. Tap into your "genius within" to create inspiring ideas that strengthen your belief in the possibility of success in your life, and fill your "motivation tanks". Plan to sustain your motivation by staying focused on your vision, reminding yourself of past success, and remembering that if another person can do it, so can you. Finally, take the option of quitting off your table, and make a commitment worthy of your vision.

Chapter Eight

COMMON SENSE PLANNING

"Planning doesn't have to be elaborate, difficult or perfect, and it's not vital to success. Action is vital to success. Planning is just a tool – nothing more, nothing less."

Just as it's important for you to define your own terms for success, you must also define your own terms for what constitutes a plan, and base your plan on what makes sense for you. I honestly don't know who came up with the idea that a person can't possibly succeed without an excruciatingly detailed plan; one that includes every teeny, tiny detail and explores every possible scenario, with projections for each. Regardless of who the person was, the notion that a detailed plan is vital to success is absolutely ridiculous.

There is no such thing as a perfect plan. It's amazing how many people believe that a plan must be perfect before they can take action and succeed. Have you ever known someone who was so bogged down in the planning process that they never seemed to get anything done? [Politicians are notorious for this.] Or maybe you know someone who decided to change their goals, because they were worried that what they really wanted to do would require elaborate planning. Well, planning doesn't have to be elaborate, difficult or perfect, and it's not vital to success. Action is vital to success. Planning is just a tool – nothing more, nothing less.

Think Easy

Planning is something we all do, whether we are aware of the process or not, from the simplest task to the most complex. We make plans every day – what clothes to wear, what time to leave for work, who's going to pick the kids up after school, what to eat for dinner, who's going to do the dishes, and what time to go to bed. Simple tasks we perform every day are planned quickly, almost instantly in our mind. With barely a thought we plan what we want, what we'll do, how we're going to do it, and when it has to be done – quick and easy.

Planning how to spend a weekend usually takes a little longer, but again, can be easily worked out in our mind. Planning a vacation may require more time, maybe a little paper to write down information about travel and lodging, with some coordination for both – reservations, check-in time, how many nights-stay, when to leave, travel by car, bus train or plane, and what route to take. Regardless of the specific task, figuring out how and when we are going to accomplish something (planning) is part of our daily lives.

When contemplating the development of your strategic plan to accomplish the tasks that support the achievement of your goals and the realization of your vision, approach the idea with common sense. You have your own unique style of getting things done. You make plans everyday, and whether you are someone who does most of the planning in your head, or someone who needs to write everything down, make sure you stay true to your own constitution. Make it easy. Take it easy.

Understanding Strategy

The concept of strategic planning is to consider different options, or different ways to get a thing done, while considering the effect each option will have on your future success (which option, being considered, brings you closer to the realization of your vision?), and then selecting the best option. Simply stated, strategy is looking ahead in anticipation of the outcome, or learning to "look before you leap".

As you move forward, making plans and taking action, consider how you can use strategy to enhance your results. When you develop ideas for how you are going to get something done, be sure to take a strategic "look before you leap". Consider the quality of the idea by asking the following questions:

1. Do I like the idea?
2. Can I see myself doing it?
3. Can I anticipate the outcome?
4. Does it bring me closer to realizing my vision?
5. Is there a better idea at this time?

By using this simple method you will begin to develop the ability to think strategically (looking ahead for what might come next). This ability will aid you in choosing more effective options that compliment other areas of your life, and that are consistent with your definition of success.

Plan Your Work

It's time now to finish creating your own *Strategic Plan*. I say "finish" because you've already done most of the work. You have established your vision, identified your goals and some tasks necessary to achieve them. You've made a decision to take action, and committed to continue taking action until what you intend to create has been completed. All that's left to do is put the finishing touches on.

Step One:

Take your *Outline for Success* and give each task a strategic look. You may decide to add more tasks, or revise, remove or replace some tasks. When you are satisfied with the quality of your ideas, move on to step two.

Step Two:

Get a calendar. Set a deadline for each task, writing down the date you expect the task to be completed. Be realistic about your ability, and give yourself a reasonable amount of time to complete each task. Arrange the tasks in order, beginning with what you want to complete first. When you are finished, move on to step three.

Step Three:

Identify any tasks that rely on someone, or something else. For example: If one of your tasks is to record music onto your computer and save it on disk, but you don't know how to burn a CD, then that task relies on learning how to burn a CD, or finding someone who can do it for you. Once you've completed this step, you will have successfully turned your *Outline for Success* into a *Strategic Plan* that will work.

That's all there is to it. Depending on what kind of person you are and what kind of goals you have, your plan may be short or long, simple or complicated. Regardless of the specific details, the one thing your plan should be is tailored to fit your unique style of getting things done. That's the common sense approach to planning. So finish up, and get ready to put your plan into action!

Chapter Nine

IMPLEMENTATION

"It's your realistic view of what you face that allows you to better identify where you are and what you need to do in order to achieve great results."

Having turned your *Outline for Success* into your *Strategic Plan*, you are now ready to get moving, to set the wheels in motion, to get your project off the ground, to shove off, to take off, to lift off, to rock and roll, to get this party started, to get busy taking action and go to work building your dream. This is the exciting part, the fun part, like the beginning of a journey when you feel the train start to move, carrying you forward as it leaves the station and you think to yourself, "I'm on my way - Destination Success!"

This leg of your journey is all about turning your ideas into action, and the beauty part is the more you do the more successful you'll become; a principle that can be applied to every aspect of your life. If you want to be healthier, exercise *more*. If you want a better relationship, pay *more* attention to your partner. If you want to communicate better, listen *more*. If you want a promotion at work, meet *more* of your company's needs. If you want to get better grades in school, study *more*. If you want to be a better musician, practice *more*. If you want to be a better parent, spend *more* time with your children. If you want to be more successful, take *more* action. Life is short. Get busy!

[Well, that just about sums up the action phase of your success journey, but there are a few more considerations that will help you better navigate your course.]

Keep it Real

Your enthusiasm and belief that you can accomplish anything are very important and vital to your success, but so is remembering that what you hope to accomplish is going to take some serious effort and will not come easy. The best approach to getting results is to combine your confidence with a realistic view of what you're up against.

In the previous chapter I mentioned there is no such thing as a perfect plan. That's because we can't see the future. We can only control our own choices. Even though we can and should try to anticipate the outcomes of our actions, we cannot expect to be right 100% of the time. We *can* expect our circumstances to change, that some of our ideas will work and some will not, and that someone or something we rely on might come through for us or might fail.

When I say "be realistic", I'm not saying "don't expect great results". On the contrary, it's your realistic view of what you face that allows you to better identify where you are and what you need to do in order to achieve great results. So keep it real.

Stay Flexible

Good plans are not set in stone. As you take the drive down the road to your success, understand you will encounter speed bumps that can slow you down, pot-holes that can knock your wheels out of alignment, and road blocks that can stop you dead in your tracks. It is for these very reasons that it's important to view your plan as a guide; an outline that provides a general direction, but is not so rigid that it can't be changed.

Successful people encounter problems as frequently as unsuccessful people do, but the difference is that successful people have plans that are fluid, allowing them to adapt to changing circumstances and to improvise different courses of action than were originally planned. It's this fluidity, or flexibility, that allows them to overcome obstacles more effectively and with greater success. As you move forward, understand that in order to overcome obstacles there might be times when it's necessary to alter your plan. If what you originally planned doesn't work, do something else. Flexibility is the key.

How Do You Eat an Elephant?

Sometimes the plans we make or the tasks we want to perform can seem enormous and overwhelming, so much so that we don't know where to begin. Feeling overwhelmed with the enormity of a project can lead to putting off getting started, stopping shortly after we've started, finding other things to do instead, or never getting started at all. The project just seems too big to handle, and therefore impossible to achieve. So why bother starting something that can't be done?

This line of thinking occurs more often than we expect, and is something that most of us have or will struggle with at some point in our lives. The key to overcoming this obstacle is to make our plans workable by breaking up larger tasks into small parts that we can handle.

If you find yourself struggling with this issue, feeling overwhelmed with the size of your project, I would like you to try and imagine eating an elephant. That seems impossible, doesn't it? Well, I believe it *is* possible to eat an elephant, although I would agree it's a feat that could prove to be extremely difficult. Assuming it is possible to eat an elephant, the only question remaining is how? How do you eat an elephant? The answer is simple: One bite at a time.

IN A NUTSHELL

There are four steps to the successful implementation of your strategic plan:

1. GET BUSY: The more you do, the more you will achieve.

2. KEEP IT REAL: Recognize what you're up against and apply the effort required to achieve great results.

3. STAY FLEXIBLE: Be ready to adapt, improvise and make changes, when necessary, to successfully overcome obstacles.

4. EAT AN ELEPHANT ONE BITE AT A TIME: Understand the effect that feeling overwhelmed can have on your ability to take and sustain action, and keep your plan broken down into small parts you can handle.

Chapter Ten

PROBLEM SOLVING

"History will judge us not by the adversity we face, but instead by how we respond in the face of adversity."

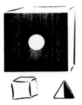

Problems are obstacles that stand between us and the realization of our vision, the achievement of our goals, or the accomplishment of various tasks we would like to perform. Unarguably, the ability to solve problems is necessary to all achievement, because achievement itself is the accumulation of obstacles which have been successfully negotiated through problem-solving.

Make a Choice

People encounter problems or face adversity every day. Adversity comes in different forms and presents different challenges for each of us, such as the loss of a job, the break-up of a marriage, the delinquency of a child, the failing of an exam, the crashing of an automobile, the diagnosis of a disease, the denial of a loan application, being passed over for a promotion, being in charge of people who don't listen, living paycheck to paycheck, facing bankruptcy, facing downsizing, facing outsourcing, etc... But it's not the problems we face that define who we are or determine how successful we ultimately become.

When we encounter problems, the first step in solving them is to make a decision to face them head on. It's normal to feel frustrated, angry, disappointed, uncertain or even scared, but how we react or respond to the problems we face is our choice. Some people avoid problems, because they can't deal with the way the problems make them feel. They go to great lengths to get out of confronting or addressing the issues that cause problems, and waste a lot of time just wishing the problems would go away. Other people get busy solving problems right away. They understand that problems don't solve themselves. In either case, how we react to problems is a choice. That's right. We have the power to choose how we are going to respond.

Successful people don't have fewer problems than unsuccessful people. We all face adversity. We all have problems. What determines our success is how we respond to the problems we face. Do we run and hide when problems arise, avoiding them and hoping they will go away, or do we face those problems head on and get busy solving them? The choice is ours. In the end, history will judge us not by the adversity we face, but instead by how we respond in the face of adversity.

Change Your Point of View

As horrible as some problems may seem, there are benefits we realize as a result of working through the problem-solving process. Every cloud really does have a silver lining.

When I look back on all the problems I faced in my own life, I realize that if I had never encountered those problems and worked to solve them, I would not be as capable as I am today. I now understand that every problem I solve makes me a stronger person, and better at something. I learn from mistakes, gain experience, become more aware, become more productive, gain confidence, and feel more successful. As a result, my view of what a problem is has changed over the years. I find myself looking at problems from a completely different angle – a different point of view. I don't see them as problems anymore.

From this new perspective, instead of seeing problems, I see opportunities for improvement. When my children aren't behaving, I see the opportunity to become a better parent. When my wife and I aren't communicating, I see the opportunity to become a better listener. When my soccer team loses, I see the opportunity to become a better coach. When my employees lack motivation, I see the opportunity to become a better leader. When my lawn is infested with crabgrass, I see the opportunity to become a better gardener, and so on. I have found that by viewing problems as opportunities I can solve those problems more effectively, and with greater results than I could in the past.

So the next time you are faced with a problem, I encourage you to step back and observe that problem from a different angle. Look at it from a different point of view. Look for the silver lining, and recognize the opportunity for improvement.

Three Easy Steps

The process for effectively solving problems, overcoming obstacles, or making the most of your opportunities has three easy steps.

Step One:

Find the real problem. Investigate the problem and do your best to figure out what is really going on. Ask questions (Who? What? Where? When? Why?). Many problems can often be traced back to the same cause or real problem. For example:

A company is experiencing a decrease in sales, an increase of customer complaints, increased expenses, and high turnover. At first glance it might appear that this company has four different problems that need solving, but in reality it has only one problem. If you guessed low employee morale, you are on the right track, but not quite there. Low employee morale is contributing to the other four problems, but what is causing employee morale to be low? Answer that question and you get to the heart of the matter – the real problem. Once the cause of low employee morale is identified a suitable solution can be worked out, and by improving employee morale the company can reduce turnover, lower its costs, improve customer service, and increase sales.

As you can see, many problems have one source (the real problem), and the key to finding that source is asking questions. Simply ask questions until you feel you've uncovered the real problem; then move on to the next step.

Step Two:

Make a list of possible solutions. Write down what you could do, or how you could do something differently in order to solve the problem. Now turn what you *could* do into what you *will* do by taking your list through the three steps of common sense planning covered in chapter eight.

Step Three:

Implement your solution.

That's all there is to it. Understanding that problems are a part of life, learning to view problems as opportunities, and getting busy solving those problems using this simple, three step approach will help you overcome obstacles more effectively, and with greater results.

Chapter Eleven

BALANCE

"Maintaining balance is vital to the accomplishment of your long term goals and the realization of a true and lasting success."

The need for balance is evident all around us, in nature, in music, in sports, in business and everywhere else we look. In order for a garden to grow, it needs the right balance of fertilizer, sun, shade, and water. In order for an orchestra to produce beautiful music, it needs the right balance of instruments, rhythm, melody, and harmony. In order for a team to win, it needs the right balance of offense, defense, individual skill, and teamwork. In order for a business venture to be successful, it needs the right balance of supply, demand, sales, and profitability.

Achieving great results requires balance, and taking a good look within ourselves should produce that same evidence. In order for us to grow, produce something beautiful, to win, and be successful realizing our dreams, we need to find the right balance in our own lives between work, family, friends, and community. In order to achieve real success, we need to keep our balance physically, emotionally, intellectually, and spiritually.

Understanding is the Key

Balance is a state of being, a combination of all the aspects of your life, that when put together, leave you with a sense of rightness, fulfillment and happiness. When you feel happy, confident, upbeat and positive, like you're on the right track, like everything's coming up roses, like nothing can stop you now or like all is right with the universe – that's balance.

Understanding is the key to achieving balance in your life – understanding who you are, what you want, where you are going, and how you are going to get there. By reading, and working through *Take Charge – Get Results* to this point, you have been deepening your understanding of these very things.

You have redefined success on your own terms, and put on the right sized boots. You understand the meaning of leadership, and have decided to take charge. You have unleashed your desire, raised your self awareness, and established a vision for your life. You have a sense of purpose, and have made a decision to act. You have set goals, and outlined your success. You believe in the possibility of your success, and have made a real commitment. You have turned your outline for success into a strategic plan, and decided to get busy implementing your plan. You understand that problems are a part of life, and have made a choice to face problems head on. You have done all these things, and as a result, not only do you have the understanding necessary to make good decisions and take action that is consistent with your true self, but you have the understanding to achieve real balance as well.

Sometimes we achieve balance by design, and sometimes we achieve balance by accident. Regardless of how it's achieved, to have balance in our lives is a very good feeling. Wouldn't it be terrific, from this point forward, to sustain that feeling of balance, that rightness with the universe? You bet it would! Maintaining balance is vital to the accomplishment of your long-term goals and the realization of a true and lasting success. The good news is you can learn to maintain your balance with the right amount of focus and effort. You already understand the need for balance, know what balance is, and know how to achieve it, so learning to maintain your balance is the next logical step.

Maintaining Balance

Life experience is a good teacher, and there are lessons to be learned in everything we do. To gain insight into how we might better maintain balance in life, let's examine a failed attempt at log crossing and consider how to apply any lessons learned. In this exercise, you'll be the one walking across the log, so prepare your mind, get ready, and visualize the following:

You survey the log, noting the width and surface condition, and identify potential obstacles where it looks slick or has branches sticking up that could cause you to trip. You choose a strategy for how to place your feet, either to place one foot in front of the other or to walk across with your toes pointing outward, so as to give you more stability. You then step onto the log and begin to move across, slowly, arms slightly outstretched, making sure you stay centered and balanced on the log as you move forward.

As you approach the halfway point, just as your confidence is growing, you think to yourself, or maybe somebody watching you says, "Don't look down!" And then what happens? You look down, of course.

As your body begins to tilt heavily to one side, your arms shoot straight out, your knees bend sharply, your butt shoots out in the opposite direction for counterbalance, and for one brief moment, you smile as you feel your weight come back to center over the log. Just enough time for a mental, "Whew, that was close!" before you realize your weight still has momentum from the counterbalancing butt-shot you so skillfully employed just seconds earlier.

Suddenly, you snap to attention, jerk your butt back over the log, lock your knees, dig your toes in and strain with all your might, hoping to freeze and stabilize your position of balance atop the log. You know, instinctively, that staying on the log requires you to maintain your balance, and that in order to maintain your balance you must be centered over the log. If you didn't know that before, you certainly know it now.

You strain with all your might to stop your body from swinging to the other side of the log, and just as you think you have it under control, your shoulders begin to tip. It's almost like slow motion, the way a tree that's being cut down begins to fall, and off in the distance, somewhere deep in your mind, you hear a logger yelling, "Timmmberrr!"

Physically, there is not much you can do at this point, because your last maneuver has left you with your toes curled, knees locked, legs straight, and arms sticking straight out. *You're as stiff as a board, and are sure to fall off the log if you don't act quickly. So before your second shoulder makes it past center, you do the only thing you can at this point; you twist your upper body sideways.*

Now you have your feet and legs facing forward, your upper body turned sideways, your arms sticking straight out, a little less stiff, but still tilting past center. If this isn't bad enough, you've begun to bend at the waist. You may have realized by now that you are in trouble, and that some major adjustments are required if you are going to stay on the log.

At this point, you decide to change your footing. With one quick jump you turn both feet so they are facing in the same direction as your upper body, and now you feel better having all of you lined up again. But you still have some problems; you are still bending at the waist, and although you have regained forward momentum, you are facing sideways on the log.

Now you are back to bending your knees and thrusting your butt backwards in a grotesquely awkward, and not very effective counter-balancing maneuver. Suddenly, you remember you have arms, and with that, begin to swing them, slowly at first, then faster, now frantically, wildly, spinning them like airplane propellers, in hopes of flying back into position on the log, but that doesn't work either.

Finally, you realize you have completely lost your balance. There you are, perched in the middle of a log, toes curled, bent over at the waist, head down, arms flailing, butt sticking up in the air, and knowing you're about to fall.

Can you relate to the experience of walking on a log and falling off about half way across? Have you ever seen someone doing the "funky chicken" while they struggled to keep their balance? Has your life ever felt like being up on that log?

Let's compare your walk across the log with your walk through life to find the similarities.

- Surveying the log, identifying obstacles and developing a strategy for how to successfully get to the other side is similar to looking at your life, determining what you want, where you are going and making a plan for how to get there. The log represents the path you've chosen.

- Taking your eyes off of where you're going, when you're half way across the log, is similar to getting distracted by things that cause you to lose sight of your vision.

- Regaining your balance on the log, only to lose it again as the momentum from your counter-balancing butt-shot pulls you off balance in the other direction, is similar to overcompensating for problems by taking extreme measures that create a whole new series of problems.

Easy as 1, 2, 3

There are three keys to maintaining balance. These simple concepts will help you achieve a higher degree of success in every area of your life.

1. Choose Your Path

- Know what you want, and where you are going. Then develop a plan (a road map) for how to get there. Following a specific path will keep you from leaning too heavily in the wrong direction.

2. Don't Look Down

- Ignore distractions that pull focus away from your vision. Keep your eyes on where you are going.

3. Make Small Adjustments

- If you begin to feel yourself losing balance, instead of over-reacting, be thoughtful in your approach. Take a step back, recognize your need for balance, and re-focus on your vision. Then make minor corrections, and bring yourself gently back into balance.

As you move forward, understand and recognize your need for balance. Seek to achieve the right balance for your life (physical, emotional, intellectual, spiritual, work, home, community, family, and friends) by knowing who you are, what you want, where you're going, and how you're going to get there.

Let life be your teacher, and maintain your balance by applying what lessons you learn. Choose your path, stay focused on your vision, and make small adjustments. It's that simple. And if you should fall, pick yourself up, dust yourself off, take what you can learn, and get back on your log.

Chapter Twelve

TAKING OWNERSHIP

"The very nature of ownership brings about a conscious mind-set focused on the best possible performance for the care and protection of an investment."

I applaud you for making it this far! If you are still reading, there can be no doubt as to the extent of your determination to succeed.

The subject of this chapter, and the final ingredient necessary for your success, is learning how to take ownership so you can get the results you're looking for. That is after all what you want, isn't it? To get results?

Understanding Ownership

The concept of ownership – to have or hold as property – is easy to understand. However, as it relates to success, ownership is not the physical act of possessing a thing, but the mind-set that occurs as a result of being the owner. It's important to understand how this mind-set impacts the quality of results. For example: Who takes better care of a business, the owner or the part-time employee? Who takes better care of a house, the owner or the renter? Who takes better care of a car, the owner or the friend who's just borrowed it?

What do you say to your friend before you hand him your car keys? You say with all seriousness, "Don't scratch the car!" What does your friend say when he returns the car? He says with a deliberate attempt at minimizing the extent of damage, "It's only a *tiny* scratch. You can *barely* see it!" all the while, holding his nearly touching thumb and forefinger in front of his squinting eye, to show you just what he means by tiny.

Obviously, owners take better care of their possessions than non-owners do. People care more about things they own because they've spent their hard-earned money to get those things. Owners have a vested interest in the things they've purchased, and have a strong desire to protect their investment. The very nature of ownership brings about a conscious mind-set focused on the best possible performance for the care and protection of an investment. Simply stated, people who own something will do a better job caring for it than those who do not.

When considering the way in which people care for their own property, it's not difficult to understand how the mind-set of ownership influences decisions, and impacts feelings of responsibility. Do you take good care of the things you own? Do you feel it's your responsibility to make decisions that result in the protection of your property? Of course you do. That's easy.

What if you were to make a decision that resulted in damage to your property? Would you continue exercising the same bad judgment, or would you make a better decision? If you kept lending your car to a friend, and he kept returning it with scratches, would you continue lending your car to that friend? Of course you wouldn't. Your sense of ownership wouldn't allow you to.

On the Defensive

Understanding what it means to take ownership of property is easy, because it is something that all of us do. Understanding what it means to take ownership of results however is not so easy, because it is something that many of us don't do. In fact many of us have, and continue to do just the opposite.

Have you ever heard someone, who just failed at something, make a statement like this? "I did everything perfect, and it still didn't work out!" or this? "I tried everything I could think of. It's just impossible!" or this? "Don't look at me. I did everything just the way you told me to!" or this? "If it wasn't for "so and so", everything would have been fine!" Have *you* ever made any statements like these?

When things don't turn out the way we want them to, it's quite normal for us to find fault with something or someone else. We have a built-in defense mechanism designed to keep us from feeling bad about ourselves. When we experience results that are less than satisfying, our defense mechanism goes to work conjuring up all sorts of reasons why it's not our fault, so we can get back to feeling good about ourselves as quickly as possible.

It's like the student who gets a bad grade and blames the teacher for being boring, instead of blaming herself for not studying. Or like the coach who, after a tough loss, blames his players for not executing the game plan, instead of blaming himself for having a weak strategy. Or like the employer who blames his employees for poor performance, instead of blaming himself for failing to train them properly. Or like the employee who tries to justify her lack of effort by saying that if her boss wasn't such a jerk, she would do a better job. Our defense mechanism is there to tell us what we want to hear, so we won't feel guilty about our failures.

The problem with this defense is that it's not entirely honest. It's similar to a Washington "Spin-Doctor". It twists and distorts the facts to support our need to be right, even when we are wrong. It clouds the view of our faults, and covers up our mistakes, which results in making those mistakes over and over again. Making repeated mistakes, and suffering repeated failures as a result of our inability to see and correct our faults, can be a real obstacle to achieving our goals. Learning to take ownership of our results is the key to overcoming this obstacle.

Honesty is the Best Policy

I bet you've heard this before! Well, it's true. It's just some of the best advice that was ever given. Honesty really is the best policy. Learning to take ownership of your results begins with learning to admit when you're wrong. Don't be defensive. Don't listen to your "Spin-Doctor". In fact, fire him! Send him packing! Get rid of him – he's bad news! Always, always, always be honest with yourself!

To take ownership of results means to acknowledge the role you play, to confess, or own up to your part in the quality of an outcome (good or bad). That is to say, recognizing how your actions contributed to the success or failure of an outcome, and then accepting responsibility for those actions.

No-Fault Insurance

Any time an auto accident occurs there is always someone at fault. Maybe one person is more at fault than the other, or maybe the blame is fifty-fifty. Sometimes other factors contribute to the accident like bald tires, bad brakes or dangerous road conditions. Whatever the case, the great thing about no-fault insurance is that all of the parties involved take care of their own damage. They're covered, no matter who's at fault. Little time is wasted on determining who's to blame. There's no need to argue or go to court; they just exchange a little information and they're done. Then the insurance companies spend some money, and whatever is broken gets fixed. In no time the drivers are back on the road, as if the accident never happened. Hopefully driving more careful than before, but they're back on the road nonetheless.

You see, the insurance companies realized a long time ago that by paying their own claims, instead of going to court and wasting their money fighting over who was at fault, they were able to realize much greater profits in the long run.

This same concept can be applied to protecting the quality of your results. As you work toward achieving your goals, accidents will happen that can bring about poor results. You might make a mistake. Someone you depend on might let you down. You might have to work with bad equipment or maybe you'll be thrown into a situation you're not ready for. Whatever the case, the great thing about taking ownership of your results is that *you* take care of your own damage (your own mistakes). You're covered, no matter who's at fault.

Being the owner of your results allows you to focus on *your* performance, to own up to *your* part in the outcome. You don't need to waste time arguing about who's to blame; just gather the information you need to make an accurate assessment of how your actions contributed to the poor results, and you're done. Then deal with the consequences caused by your mistake, correct whatever it is you did wrong, and in no time you'll be back on the road to success, as if those poor results never happened.

You too, can achieve greater results in the long run, once you realize (as the insurance companies did) that you need to pay your own claims.

Enjoy the Profits

Ownership is not just about admitting when you're wrong. It's also about recognizing what you've done right. Most of us don't have a problem taking credit for, or feeling good about something we've accomplished. However, sometimes we become frustrated when the achievement of a goal isn't happening fast enough, or when something doesn't go according to plan. Sometimes we stay frustrated for so long that even when we finally achieve the goal, instead of feeling a sense of accomplishment, all we can muster is a tired sense of relief. Instead of cheering and passing out High-Fives, we give a little twirl of the finger and mutter, "Whoop-de-do."

If you are going to take ownership of your results and hold yourself accountable for your mistakes, then it's only fair to recognize your accomplishments, and allow yourself to feel good about them. In fact, it is necessary. Failing to see the good in what you've done, can be just as detrimental to your success, as failing to admit your mistakes. If you are not aware of what works, how can it be duplicated?

Recognizing what you've done right (what works) does two things. First, it allows you to duplicate good results by duplicating proper action. Second and most important, it allows you to move forward with increased confidence; the kind of confidence that fuels a belief in possibilities and helps sustain a positive, "can-do" attitude.

For this reason, the next time you experience frustration with the way things are going, I encourage you to stop what you're doing and take stock of the situation. Of course you'll want to honestly acknowledge your mistakes and work to correct them, but remember, look for what you've done right. Then allow yourself to feel good about what you've accomplished to that point. The best part about ownership is enjoying the profits.

Make an Investment

Now that you understand the impact taking ownership has on results, it's time to *become* the owner of your results. It's not enough to "think" like an owner or "pretend" to be an owner. The only way you can truly own your results, and have the capacity to consider the quality of those results in a way that only an owner can, is to make an investment. You must have a personal stake in the outcome. There must be something you stand to gain if you succeed, and something you stand to lose if you fail.

Consider the work you've done so far in this book. You've defined success on your own terms, taken charge of your situation, created a vision, established your intent, set goals, begun to believe in the possibility of your success, made a commitment, planned your work, and might have already begun to implement your plan. You are ready to solve problems and understand how to maintain your balance as you move forward. So I ask you, what do you stand to gain if you succeed? What do you stand to lose if you fail?

To own property requires an investment of money. If you invest wisely, and do a good job protecting your investment you will see a return on your investment. You stand to gain more money. If however, you do not invest wisely, or do a poor job of caring for your investment, not only would you lose any future gains, but you could lose your initial investment as well.

To own results requires an investment of yourself – everything that matters to you and why – the realization of your vision, and how the achievement of your goals impacts your future sense of accomplishment, happiness and self-respect. These comprise the currency with which results are purchased. Your time, energy, and desire to succeed are your investment. The realization of your vision, or the achievement of a goal is what you stand to gain. What you stand to lose is something only you can decide. For some, it may be their future sense of accomplishment, for others their future happiness. Still others may feel their self-respect is at stake.

Whatever the case, one thing holds true for us all. How much of ourselves we have invested in an outcome will ultimately determine the degree to which we stand to gain or lose. Regardless of what you hope to accomplish in your life, in your business, or in your career, the greater your vision the more rewarding the benefits of success will be. The down side of this is that the more you hope to achieve the greater your disappointment will be if you fail. The questions you need to ask yourself now are: Is the realization of my vision *worth* pursuing? Am I *willing* to make the necessary investment? Am I *clear* on what is at stake? Am I *ready* to take ownership of my results?

Only you can answer these questions. I can only encourage you by saying that I have made the investment, and it has made all the difference in my life. Are there times when I feel disappointed in myself? Yes. Are there times when I'm not satisfied with my results? You bet. Are there times when I feel unhappy with myself? Absolutely. Would my life have been as rewarding and fulfilling as it is today had I not taken the risk? Not in a million years!

When it comes to getting results, the idea is to view those results as your property. Make an investment, and stay focused on the quality of the outcome. Approach your goals with the mind-set of an owner, and accept responsibility for your actions. As you move forward, ignore your "Spin Doctor", acknowledge the role you play with regard to each outcome (good or bad), and remember to enjoy your profits. That's what "taking ownership" is all about.

SUMMARY

Before a house can be built the foundation must be poured. Likewise, before great results can be achieved the foundation to support and facilitate the accomplishment of those results must be poured. In other words, before you can get results, you need to lay the proper groundwork of knowledge (what is it?), understanding (what does it mean?), and method (how is it applied?). How much we achieve, the quality of our results, and how fulfilling our lives ultimately become, depend on the strength of our foundation.

Finding success doesn't have to be a struggle. By following the process outlined in *Take Charge – Get Results*, you can lay the foundation for the accomplishment of your goals and the realization of your dreams.

Before you get started let's review by taking one last look at the principles discussed in each chapter.

1. **Success Redefined**: Look below the surface of your life, and determine what's important to you. Get your priorities straight, and make sure your actions are consistent with what you hope to achieve. Redefine the meaning of success in your own life by shutting out everything you've heard and seen, and listen to what your insides tell you. What size boots do *you* wear?

2. **Understanding Leadership**: Leaders are responsible for all outcomes (good or bad), not just some of the time, but all of the time. Leadership is not about giving orders, but about accepting the primary responsibility of leadership – to take charge. The common expectations of leadership – to lead, to guide, to enlighten, to direct, and to inspire action, - all stem from the acceptance of this primary responsibility. It is leadership that sets the course and provides direction for all achievement. Make a decision to take charge.

3. **Unleash Your Desire**: Desire is a powerful emotion that when properly focused, can drive one to excel and achieve uncommon results. Understand how desire affects winning, and recognize the desire within you. To successfully unleash the power of desire, you must raise your self-awareness and develop a clear vision. What do you want to be? What do you want to have? How do you want to feel? What matters most and why?

4. **Finding Inspiration**: Inspiration is the key to developing ideas that "smack of genius". In order to access your own source of inspiration you must have a sense of purpose, and develop a strong intent. Remember to complete the decision making process by turning what you "could" do into what you "will" do.

5. **Goal Setting**: Goals are critical to great achievement, should be well defined and written. Keep goal setting simple by viewing your goals as a list of tasks you will

accomplish to realize your vision. Outline your success by identifying main goals that support the realization of your vision. Then identify tasks that support the achievement of each goal.

6. **Sustaining Motivation**: Great ideas have the power to inspire and motivate us. How long we stay motivated will determine how much we ultimately achieve. Answer the question, "Why bother?" Remind yourself frequently of past success, and believe that you are capable – if another person can do it, so can you. The key to sustaining motivation is staying focused on your vision, and remaining firmly entrenched in your belief that all things are possible.

7. **Making A Commitment**: Commitment is a decision to continue taking action until what you intend to create is completed. When you work toward the realization of your dreams, the bigger the vision, the harder you test is bound to be. For most people, giving up is always an option. The key to making a strong and lasting commitment is to take the option of quitting off the table.

8. **Common Sense Planning**: It's important for you to define your own terms for what constitutes a plan, and base your plan on what makes sense for you. When contemplating the development of your strategic plan, approach the idea with common sense. Make it easy. Take it easy. Giving your ideas a strategic look helps you choose effective options that compliment other areas of

your life. There are three steps to Common Sense Planning. **1)** Take your *Outline for Success* and give each task a strategic look. **2)** Set a deadline for each task. **3)** Identify tasks that rely on someone, or something else. The one thing your plan should be is tailored to fit your unique style of getting things done.

9. **Implementation**: You're on your way – Destination Success! This leg of your journey is all about turning your ideas into action. If you want to be more successful, take *more* action. There are four steps to the successful implementation of your strategic plan. **1)** Get Busy. **2)** Keep It Real. **3)** Stay Flexible. **4)** Eat an Elephant One Bite at a Time.

10. **Problem Solving**: Achievement is the accumulation of obstacles which have been successfully negotiated through problem-solving. Make a decision to face problems head on and get busy solving them. View problems as opportunities to improve. The process for effectively solving problems has three easy steps. **1)** Find the real problem. Ask questions to figure out what is really going on. **2)** Make a list of possible solutions. Then turn what you could do into what you will do by taking your list through the three steps of common sense planning. **3)** Implement your solution.

11. **Balance**: Understanding is the key to achieving balance in your life – understanding who you are, what you want, where you are going, and how you are going to

get there. Maintaining balance is vital to the accomplishment of your long term goals and the realization of a true and lasting success. Let life be your teacher, and maintain your balance by applying what lessons you learn. Choose your path, stay focused on your vision, and make small adjustments. It's that simple.

12. **Taking Ownership**: The very nature of ownership brings about a conscious mind-set focused on the best possible performance for the care and protection of an investment. Being defensive about our mistakes leads to repeating those mistakes, and can be a real obstacle to achieving our goals. The key to overcoming this obstacle is learning to take ownership of results, which means to acknowledge the role you play, to confess, or own up to your part in the quality of an outcome (good or bad). You can achieve greater results in the long run, once you realize you need to pay your own claims.

If you are going to take ownership of your results and hold yourself accountable for your mistakes, then it's only fair to recognize your accomplishments, and allow yourself to feel good about them. The best part about ownership is enjoying the profits. To own results requires an investment of yourself. How much of yourself you have invested in an outcome will ultimately determine the degree to which you stand to gain or lose.

View your results as property. Make an investment, and stay focused on the quality of the outcome. Approach your goals with the mind-set of an owner, and accept responsibility for your actions.

With the proper foundation of knowledge, understanding, and method you too, can achieve great results. There's no end to the possibilities!

As you move forward, continue to apply your knowledge and understanding of success principles, to every aspect of your life, business or organization. Make decisions that are consistent with your definition of success. Take charge of your situation, and set your course. Establish your vision, and create inspiring ideas. Move with a sense of purpose, and make a decision to act. Outline your success by setting goals. Believe in the possibility of your own success, and stay focused on your vision. Take the option of quitting off the table. Tailor plans to fit your unique style, and use strategy that will enhance results. Then get busy. Keep it real, stay flexible, and keep your plans broken down into small parts you can handle. When you experience problems look for the silver lining, and recognize your opportunity to improve. Face problems head on, seek to discover the true source of those problems, and implement your solutions. Find your balance and maintain it. Choose your path, stay focused on where you're going, and make small adjustments. Finally, take ownership. Invest yourself in the outcome and take the risk, pouring your heart and soul into everything you hope to accomplish.

It's time for you to get started. Something is calling you. Can you hear it? It's your hopes and dreams, it's everything you want and why, it's your vision beckoning. It's calling out for *you*, and it's saying, -

"Take Charge – Get Results!"

Dare To Dream Again

You think I don't understand,
But I do.

The odds are not in our favor.
Percentage-wise, very few people achieve success.
The deck is stacked against us, and we have
Very little chance of succeeding.

It would probably be better if we just accepted reality,
And didn't try so hard to get
Something we can never have.
Just do the best we can, being average.

That's how most people think.
I know, because
I am most people,
And so are you.

My dreams have died many times.
I know the pain of failure
And the cruelty of life.
So do you.

I know the fear of rebuilding a dream.
I feel it now.
So do you.

TAKE CHARGE – GET RESULTS

I have gambled and lost.
I have played to win, and walked away in defeat.
I have stood tall,
Only to be knocked flat by Failure's merciless blow.

I have paid the price for daring to go
Just one more round with fate,
And I have cried until my soul was dry.
So have you.

If you do not dare
To dream again,
To stand and fight and try to win,
I understand.

If you lack the strength
To go on,
Then stop here and rest awhile.
I understand.

After all, I had to stop and rest too.

But now I am ready to rejoin the game,
And though my fear is great,
I will beat it down, charge with a fury,
And Fight!

I will never give up,
Not as long as there's a breath in my body!
If I get knocked down,
I'll get back up!
If my dream is destroyed,
I'll build another!

I must go on.
No matter how great the fear,
No matter what the odds,
No matter what the risk,
I must go on trying!

This is who I am.
I don't know why, but I know
I cannot change it.

And I also know this;
We are the same, you and I.

And although you still need time to rest,
It won't be long before you rise again,
And we will fight together – side by side –
Defeating our fears, and realizing our dreams.

This is who you are.
I don't know why, but I know
You cannot change it.

ABOUT THE AUTHOR

George J. Morse is an Executive Leadership Coach and the Founder / President of Morse & Associates, Inc. He has more than 20 years of leadership experience, and a proven track record of success in business. He specializes in Leadership Development, Interactive Management, Strategic Planning, Problem Solving, Organization & Efficiency, Teamwork / Team Building, Employee Motivation, Training Solutions, Conflict Resolution, Cost Controls, and Profitability. He provides coaching, consulting, training, and workshops to top-level administrators and their teams, helping them to enhance performance, and achieve greater results.

George is a devoted Husband and Father. He has been married to his wife and partner, Andrea, for more than 20 years, and they are very proud of their 3 wonderful children, Michelle, A.J., and Taylor Marie.

George also coaches individuals in the areas of Family Leadership, Parenting, Relationships, Career Planning, Budget & Finances, and Health & Fitness, helping them to live more rewarding and fulfilling lives.

He is a respected community leader who passionately believes that making the world a better place begins with building better communities. It's his strong desire, to have a positive impact on the lives of those around him, that motivates him to donate his time and money for the support of school programs, sports programs, youth activities and various service organizations.

In 1993, at the age of twenty-eight, George made his dream of becoming a business owner a reality, when he opened his first Subway restaurant. In 2000, after working together with his wife to build a successful business, he founded Morse & Associates, Inc., and added two more locations. By 2002 his company owned and operated five locations. Today his management team continues to run the company's multi-unit franchise operation, while George focuses on developing the leaders of tomorrow.

He currently resides with his family in northern Michigan.

Dear Reader,

I'm interested in hearing what you've accomplished after reading "Take Charge – Get Results, and the impact the book has made on your life or business.

If you'd like to share your story with me, please send a letter via regular mail to the address below, or e-mail your letter to george@coachmorse.com.

I encourage you to share "Take Charge – Get Results" with your colleagues, family and friends. If you wish, you may order books from me directly.

I'm available to respond to requests for coaching. For information about the services I provide you can visit my website. www.coachmorse.com

I wish you continued success on your journey!

Sincerely,

George J. Morse
Executive Leadership Coach
President, MAI

Morse & Associates, Inc.
P.O. Box 695
Oscoda, MI 48750
(989) 739-3847